Talk between the habitats Volume 2

The realm of the dragons

Susanne Edelmann

Impressum

Bibliografische Information der Deutschen Nationalbibliothek: Die Deutsche Nationalbibliothek verzeichnet diese Publikation in der Deutschen Nationalbibliografie; detaillierte bibliografische Daten sind im Internet über dnb.dnb.de abrufbar.

©2024 Susanne Edelmann
Herstellung und Verlag: BoD – Books on Demand,
Norderstedt
ISBN: 9783758375347

Content

1. Introduction 7

    1.1 "Playing with frequencies" 14

2. Welcome 23

3. Energy-based needs 28

    3.1 Holistic stability 29

    3.2 Life-enhancing frequencies 41

    3.3 Natural orders 48

    3.4 Embedded in the big picture.................. 53

4. Your individual needs 61

    4.1 Security is crucial................................. 70

    4.2 A completely essential life 77

    4.3 Inner leadership 82

5. Self-empowerment 90

    5.1 Your power lies on the energy-based level 93

    5.2 Your power is based on authenticity....... 99

6. Power 101

    6.1 Power based on your essential vibrational frequency 102

    6.2 Power based on light............................. 108

1. Introduction

In the last millennia, when a personality has incarnated as a human being, he has consciously submerged into the material-based dimension and into unconsciousness. The personality has lived as a human identity and completely forgotten who he really is.

For several years now, in some places on the planet, the fundamental vibration frequency has been so high that infants born there enter a frequency that makes fundamental immersion into unconsciousness impossible. These babies and toddlers are and behave differently than previous babies and toddlers did so far. Due to the higher fundamental vibration frequency of the environment and the parents, who also have a higher vibration frequency than is generally the case among humans, the fundamental vibration frequency of the respective infants also remains rather high right from the start. If then, the environment of said babies continues to be pleasantly healthy, the holistic frequency of the respective babies rises very quickly. At least as high as that of their immediate surroundings, their parents or even their own core being.

Said incident means that these children are consciously connected to their own essence and therefore consciously carry within themselves who they essentially are. They are also still connected to the energy-based dimension in the material-based human habitat and, depending on their personal vibration frequency, they are then even subordinate to the energy-based level, since a certain high basic vibration frequency currently leads to an involuntary connection to the energy-based dimension in all people.

The children described are clearly different and I would like to consciously recommend them to you. Because these special children benefit from people who understand them and their situation and consciously accompany them in mastering the material-based dimension in a beneficial and effective way (because they have to do that too, there is no way around it) and in finding their own essential place in human society.
Said children are visibly different. They react based on energy and they capture (also) based on energy. Thus, many currently common human behaviors lead to irritation and ultimately to a loss of relationships.
Currently, this mostly happens outside the awareness of the parents or caretakers. They only notice that the child in question is behaving significantly differently.

Most people do not yet realize why this is the
case, even if they are directly affected and could
certainly recognize it due to their own high level
of personal development.

Said child cannot take you seriously, if you are
caught up in certain fictions and behave out of
these fictions. The child grasps involuntarily.
Fictions and that which actually is. As a result,
the child in question behaves irritated and from a
purely human perspective not appropriate to the
situation. It reacts energy based. In fact, the child
mostly reacts in an energy-based manner. Also,
in the area of relationships. He does it intuitive.
And if an adult does not understand this, he will
not understand the child. Worse still, he will
pathologize said child.
Additionally, in the energy-based dimension
relationships are in a certain setting: An "I"
meets another "I". Respectfully. Both are. The
ones they are. Thus, sad child reacts instinctively
with irritation to human emotional impositions
(and as an infant and toddler you are exposed to
this behavior in large quantities in the human
environment). Thus, another situation in which
he is usually not understood. Yet, meanwhile, he
needs pure and respectful love, security and
benevolent attention in order to remain
holistically healthy.

The children I am talking about here, are all
highly developed and have certain essential
responsibilities here, on planet Earth. They want
to perform these tasks as quickly as possible, but
they first have to master all human and material-
based tasks. And this requires very conscious,
mindful and respectful support. It requires adults
who have successfully mastered it themselves,
can grasp the truth and are able to neither
exaggerate nor devalue, but instead give space
without judgment and grant these children the
greatest possible independence.

However, said child also needs helpful human
role models in everyday human life, in order to
learn and understand how to move in the human
environment. Even if it is transparently recorded
and known. Especially then. The child must know
that what he is doing is correct and he has
correctly grasped, even if most of the people
around him are different, perceive things
differently and, in particular, often behave
incongruently and extremely unhealthy.
He learns through observation and his own
experiences, and it helps him if you are aware of
this. He also communicates very often in an
energy-based manner and his own inner
essential self will repeatedly benefit from the
experiences stored in your personal energy
space.

In particular, said child must be aware of the effects of forms of energy and complex frequencies and consciously learn to deal with them in a beneficial way. However, he also has to get to know the aspect of superimpositions and projections and here too, he has to be accompanied in independent, ongoing dissolution work. In addition, the child also benefits if he learn to master duality at an early age and are no longer at the mercy of it.

Said child needs energy-based teachers who understand the child's irritations (especially the legitimacy of the irritation), who repeatedly formulate the differences between the two dimensions, who accompany him through the unhealthy "jungle" of human behavior, structures and norms, and at the same time, gives the child a lot of freedom in shaping his own environment and his own everyday life.

A child who meets the criteria just described does not need an adult to tell him what is right or wrong. However, he still needs a mentor who will support him in becoming confident in himself and in having the courage to find the right solutions for himself. A mentor who helps him find his way, as he is always a human child. Despite at best a highly developed core of being.

Over the next few decades, the number of children described will increase. On the one hand, they can find their way into their essential tasks much more quickly and thus contribute to the current "Project Earth". On the other hand, however, they are absolutely dependent on an environment that is capable of understanding and accompanying them, otherwise they are often damaged, pathologized and thwarted.

We are currently looking for people who are able and willing to take on the task described. Please consciously check within yourself and if you have a "YES", formulate this consciously and clearly and you will be guided accordingly.
At the same time, I would like to point out to you that the task described is an energy-based task and you can and will only carry it out if you are appropriately capable. Please examine consciously and you will know.
If you are capable and have received the appropriate higher-level permission, your practical life in the next few weeks and months will be completely focused on the relevant preparatory work. We need you. Very quickly. However, you are only helpful if you are appropriately prepared.

At the same time, as part of this task, you will learn a lot about the differences between the material-based and energy-based dimensions, and whatever you learn while practically carrying out the task, will serve you in many ways in global intercultural communication. However, you are also a pioneer in this task, and it helps you, if you are aware of this and know that you will naturally not succeed in everything right from the start

This book is largely written by the council of the energy-based realm of the dragons. Like the realm of the elves, they also consciously make a certain area of their realm available. And in their area, there is also a place for conscious exchange. This place is currently aimed primarily at those people who take on the task just described. Dragons have always had a very close connection to humans and the material-based living space. They currently live in the seventh dimension. At the same time, they are very familiar with the differences between the individual dimensions on planet Earth and in particular with how energy-based evolution works in the context of Earth. They will therefore be able to support you in many ways. Additionally, you can meet other people doing the same task at the described location.

Before I "hand over the microphone to the council of the energy-based realm of the dragons", I would like to point out a few aspects that can currently be helpful to you in your everyday life, but also in the task just mentioned.

1.1 "Playing with frequencies"

If you are highly developed and fully conscious again, and have mastered the third, fifth and seventh dimensions in this one human life, energy-based evolution is fully available to you. Something that those people who already have access to this ability are currently too little aware of. If energy-based evolution is fully available to you, you use vibration and frequencies to design, change or shape. An effortless and beautiful form of action that suits you once you discover it and use it consciously.

- If you lower the frequency slightly, you stabilize the respective setting.
- If you increase the frequency slightly, you support cleansing and clarification and thereby promote truth, healing and strengthening.

Over time you will discover that you can consciously increase or decrease your own vibration frequency. This with the aim of having a corresponding effect in your respective environment. However, you can also dampen your own vibration frequency using (dark) colors or (synthetic) materials or increase its height (and power) using (light) colors and (natural) materials.

If you consciously let go and allow your own inner essential self to introduce you to the topic, you will experience that your wardrobe begins to fill with different colors and materials. Colorfully mixed. Far away from current fads, mental constructs or any recommendations. If you also consciously engage with the topic and consciously let guide yourself in your choice of clothing, you will find that you are being guided very clearly internally. You usually don't know what you're going to wear the night before, but in the morning it's usually very clear. And if you like, let your own inner essential self consciously explain to you why you are wearing what you are wearing. Now, your clothes also serves additional aspects and it helps you, if you are fully aware of this.

If you are attentive, you will be able to observe that you can (somewhat) change your own vibration frequency with your food intake. Short-term and minimal, but still effective. If you eat earth vegetables, meat or industrially processed food, you lower your own vibration frequency and thereby stabilize yourself (if necessary) and sometimes also your immediate surroundings. If you eat natural, unprocessed fruits (or fruit vegetables), this increases the power of your high vibration frequency.

If you now accompany a child who begins his human incarnation in the interface between the material-based and the energy-based dimension, you will be able to observe that he will intuitively use the "game of frequencies" described. This means that they must be able to decide freely and, in particular, without judgment, what clothes they wear and when they eat what food. Independent of common human ideas. Once "McDonalds and plastic toys" and once "organic apples from our own garden and light linen clothing". Other times maybe a mixture of "both and". Completely suitable at all times, viewed from an energy-based perspective.

The energy-based behavior of a child (or even an adult, where it is usually less questioned) is very often incomprehensible from a purely human, material-based perspective because it clearly cannot be classified into common patterns and norms. It is based on energy-based laws and therefore cannot be understood from a purely material-based perspective. It doesn't fit (from a purely material perspective). And this usually irritates and strengthens the efforts of the parents or those responsible for raising children to support (or even push) the child to change and thereby become suitable. Yet, that is not the goal, in said situation.

At the same time, with the behavior described they strengthen an inner basic feeling of the child of being wrong, of not being able to trust themselves, of not being understood and of fundamentally not fitting in. And so, the children described benefit from highly developed and completely conscious adults who can grasp and benevolently leave things behind.

It is always value-free and can always be different. Far from cognitive classification, control or organization. An immense challenge, especially for committed parents who want to do well and right with their child.

The story described is extremely damaging for the child himself. Especially when his holistic being connects to the energy-based level. Because now the following applies: His inside creates his outside. And so, the fundamental inner insecurity described, but also the beliefs that emerged in childhood, will shape accordingly. Regardless of whatever is done on a material basis. Energy-based evolution works. Usually without the child or those around them being aware of what is actually happening.
The child is at the mercy of the mechanisms, to a certain extent. His life is now shaped based on energy, without him being able to influence it voluntarily. Especially when no one outside teaches and supports him to liberate himself sustainably and thereby achieve actual self-empowerment.

Yet, if one or the other resonates with you and it feels right for you, put the book aside and allow your previous biography to open up to you from the aspects described. So that you can recognize and understand things even better.

The child described is not "holy" and so, it is extremely important not to treat him excessively or in any other way "specially". He is still (also) a human child and must learn to live this role well and beneficially. He must learn to behave appropriately in human society, to calmly withdraw when necessary and to subordinate himself to official authorities and to root himself and his own life very well in human society. During his current incarnation, he will always be a "completely normal person" and this needs to be learned very consciously under the circumstances described. Said child must learn to feel "comfortable" in his human body, to control his emotions at all times and to carry out his human tasks in a disciplined manner.
The child benefits from very conscious parental guidance, awareness and attentiveness. He carries a human part within him that is at a child's level of development and this part requires conscious external guidance and support, even when the essential self is highly developed and freely present in conscious power.

However, the accompaniment and support of the children described will ideally be significantly different than that of the average child and we hope that as many of these children as possible will be accompanied by people who are fully aware and capable.
But regardless of whether you carry out this task or not, you will benefit from letting your own inner essential self show you the "play of frequencies" very consciously and thereby understanding it comprehensively.

If you live as a human in the interface between material-based and energy-based dimensions, you have material-based human needs, but you also have energy-based needs. As an adult, you have up to this point gone through a more or less conscious path of becoming completely conscious and, through your conscious engagement with the new circumstances, you have usually intuitively discovered that you now also have energy-based needs. The children described also have this. However, they usually cannot formulate accordingly and therefore need adults in their immediate environment who know, if necessary, formulate and consciously support.

Energy-based needs mean, among other things, that you need certain frequencies or forms of energy here and now, so that you are fully comfortable or can fulfill certain tasks. And if you like, let your own inner, essential self introduce you to the topic very consciously and consciously show you what this can mean in practical terms in your current everyday life. Start consciously paying attention to frequencies. Pay attention to how they affect you and your well-being. Let your own inner essential self show you how you can influence them yourself. And let him explain to you, which frequencies shape which human topics. The topic of frequencies is a large and extremely exciting area and once you understand it in depth, it will be extremely helpful to you in many ways.
Please be aware, however, that insights open up according to a person's level of development and integrity. Basically. A person can only grasp what he is naturally capable of.

Energy-based needs and their fulfillment are subject to one's own inner essential self, and so, they cannot be defined externally. At the same time, an infant (or toddler) cannot yet meet their needs themselves and is absolutely dependent on adults to do this for them. If you now, begin to consciously include the energy-based needs, this means that you are bringing the child into contact with the frequencies and energies that it needs here and now.

You not only provide him with clothing, food, attention and support offers, you also provide him with frequencies and energies. In order to do this, however, you must be familiar with the topic described and ideally, you should practice this on and with yourself.

We will be publishing a book on the topic of "Project Earth" in the near future and will delve deeper into the topic described here. And so, I close the slot and hand over to the council of the energy-based realm of the dragons.

2. Welcome

Greetings!

We are pleased to be able to write this book and thereby come into conscious contact with you. If you like, allow yourself to capture the energy signature of our realm and once you have it, consciously immerse yourself in it with the aim of getting to know us and our realm. Although we live in the seventh dimension of the planet, we are still very connected to the materially based third dimension, the nature there and the people there. Your living space is significantly different than ours and at the same time, it has the potential to be an incredibly beautiful and rich living space. However, a lot has to change in this living space.

For a long time, we thought that people would make change on their own. Maybe we were a little too busy with ourselves and shifted the responsibility a little too much onto people. And so, we are very happy about the attentive veto from the realm of the elves, and it became clear to us very quickly that we would like to provide helpful support in the human habitat. Especially those people who are currently carrying a lot in the sustainable change work there.

The human environment will need a lot of energy-based teachers in the next few decades. The relevant training and specific support must be established in the human environment itself. Nevertheless, we would like to support the strengthening, training and further education of these people, especially now, when nothing in this regard is yet available. The elves have encouraged a conscious exchange with the aim of finding solutions. We would like to offer this too. At the same time, however, we would also like to be able to support you in understanding the various dimensions even better and, in particular, in using the influence of the individual dimensions on the human living space in a targeted, positive way.

As an energy-based teacher, you need a lot of knowledge and diverse skills and if you know within yourself that you will be working in this role in the near future, consciously allow everything you need for your task to flow to you in the next few months. Please consciously deal with everything that comes your way and allow yourself to fully understand each of them. In connection with your task as an energy-based teacher or as a mentor for the children mentioned in the first chapter.
Both tasks are extremely demanding, and you will only be able to carry them out, if you are sufficiently capable and prepared.

And if you know within yourself that your life will
continue in this direction, your human mind may
become restless because it has no clear idea of
this direction and cannot create it mentally. You
are always human and even if you will now take
on more and more novel / essential tasks, your
human aspects should always be completely
comfortable.
Your human mind needs images and ideas that
convey security and well-being. And your human
self needs the clear knowledge that you are
always abundantly supplied with everything you
need. Consciously allow both needs to be taken
into account and in the next few days you will
receive clear inner images of your next months
and years.
You don't need to know every detail, but you
need to know a general idea. Yet, your human
part needs information regarding housing, life,
professional and private integration and holistic
care. You carry a lot, and so, it seems particularly
important to us that your human parts are very,
very comfortable. Here and now, and also in the
coming months and years.

If you like, put the book aside for a while and let
your own inner essential self show you in detail
how your human parts can be calm and secure,
and you thus can concentrate fully on your
essential tasks.

If you then, have the secure inner foundation discussed, you will realize how extremely important it is for you in the next few months. If you experience complete security, you can fully engage with what you are now continually encountering. These are all situations that contain a variety of information that is important to you.

Allow yourself to fully grasp in each case, pay attention to your respective frequencies, the energies that surround you and, in particular, let yourself be shown how to embed yourself into the human material-based living space.
If you are completely prepared, you will now experience a kind of "holistic preparation, training and further education" for your next important task.
A phase that lasts until you are confident and well prepared. Yet, a phase that honestly takes you out of your current human life so that you can fully concentrate on your personal development.
You won't lose anything, after the time described everything will go back to normal and then, form according to your new tasks. No one outside will notice what you are walking through. However, you will benefit maximally. Please feel free, as often as it feels right for you, to travel to the place that we have prepared for this in our realm and to engage in conscious exchange with us there and to be consciously supported.

You can orient yourself to the energy signature of the place and travel there independently by making a conscious decision. If the journey serves you, it will open up to you. If it doesn't open to you, you can assume that a visit is currently not serving you.

Journey to the realm of the dragons
Retreat to a quiet, beautiful and undisturbed place, make yourself comfortable there and breathe in and out consciously and deeply a few times. If you are ready, allow yourself to be accompanied to the said place. You know when you're there. Take enough time to arrive safely and to familiarize for the first time. You will see some kind of building on your left. If you are ready, go into the building-like structure and find the right place for you inside.
If you are ready again, allow to happen for your own highest and best. You know when it's complete. Say goodbye and thank you and return to your own place by making a conscious decision. Once there, consciously stabilize yourself and rest a bit so that what you have just experienced can be integrated holistically.

And if you like, allow your current biography to be shown to you in greater depth so that you can grasp and understand it even better. A lot of practical experience in this regard will be helpful to you on behalf of your future tasks. You can ultimately only grasp in depth what you have experienced practically on your own.
At the same time, events that have not yet been fully processed can show themselves to you so that you can resolve them sustainably and thereby become completely free.

3. Energy-based needs

You yourself live in the midst of the material-based and energy-based dimensions and in the future, you will support other people in finding their way into this very demanding challenge. At the same time, you first have to be completely familiar with this very complex matter. You will find suggestions and support in this regard in several books by Susanne and her team. In this book, we would like to emphasize something that, in our opinion, has not found enough space in the previous books. It is these, the energy-based needs, that are now taking up more and more space in your life and being.

3.1 Holistic stability

People have a natural need for stability, and they usually do a lot to achieve it. As a rule, they behave in a human, materially based manner and consciously ensure that their appearance, or at least that which is important to them, is stable and remains so. At the same time, a lot of people are extremely unstable inside and if you walk through your everyday life and consciously look around, you will easily be able to determine how strong the need for stabilization currently exists in the human living space. Cell phone, media consumption, nicotine and food; they all stabilize, on a human level. All four are easily accessible in the Western world and are used very frequently. At the same time, all four have significant side effects, are also not sustainable and are more likely to be harmful in the long term.

Many people are not very connected to themselves, and many are currently taking the easiest route by doing what others are doing. People live many harmful lifestyles, and on the one hand they know this, but on the other hand they are not prepared to consciously search and consciously change.
And when we talk about "people" here, we mean a broad mass, knowing that there are also other people who are certainly searching and changing.

From a holistic perspective, it is usually (unconscious) feelings that destabilize.

And we would like to encourage you to take the topic with you into your everyday human life, to consciously observe it and just as consciously to allow yourself to be guided and instructed by your own inner essential self.

From an energy-based perspective, feelings are forms of energy and so, you can always look at them in an energy-based way and deal with them in an energy-based way. Strong feelings can be very destabilizing. Human first incarnations in particular are usually surprised and are often overwhelmed by the holistic power of human feelings. Feelings are therefore a challenge that a person must learn to deal with very consciously. On a material-based level in the form of feelings. On an energy-based level in the field of energy forms. Both are and both are at the same time. If you push feelings down and pretend, they don't exist, they remain stuck in your personal energy space on an energy-based level in the form of energy forms and then increasingly weigh you down over the course of your life. If you give them space and attention in an uncontrolled manner, they can gain so much strength that you suddenly lose control and hurt others with emotional outbursts.

**Children need role models
those with their own feelings
can deal with it in a beneficial way.
Human and energy based.**

Many people don't show their feelings externally and think they have found a good and healthy way to deal with this behavior. They control their feelings, repress or disregard them and trust their rationality. In the long term, however, this behavior is not good for them, as they lose access to their own authentic here and now feelings and thus to their personal inner navigation. The basis of their natural self-determination, viewed from an energy-based perspective.

The repressed feelings are also deposited more and more in your holistic energy field and weigh down and shape the course of your life. A little more every year. From an energy-based perspective, the variety and multitude of deposited (mostly negative) forms of energy prevent a holistically stable inner foundation and thereby promote fundamental inner insecurity. At the same time, stored forms of energy prevent direct contact with the respective authentic here and now feelings and thus, from an energy-based perspective, the power to independently shape the respective here and now.

The increasing inner instability must now be compensated for more and more externally, or it will be sunk into the unconscious through distraction or repression. Yet, it's still there, and so, the basic feelings of dependency and helplessness usually intensify.
This in turn reinforces coping strategies that are already in use or the search for external solutions.

The solution is always there
in people themselves.

The energy-based need for holistic stability is central and as one's inner essential self begins to gain power in a human life, it will first ensure that the stored forms of energy are sustainably released from the personal energy space. This happens by meeting people who also carry the said form of energy and thus trigger their own form of energy.
The feeling of degradation, for example.
You meet a person and notice the feeling of degradation in them. It touches you very much. And if you don't start acting out and making sure that he experiences dignity, but instead stay very close to yourself, you will realize that you know the feeling based on your own experiences.

If you now consciously give the said feeling space within yourself, you will have the opportunity to consciously process your own unprocessed experiences and thereby consciously resolve them. Once you have permanently resolved the feeling, you will no longer feel an inner mission to change the outside. Yet, you will still change. Based on clear inner impulses. Much more powerful than before. But you will experience this for yourself.

People are very externally oriented creatures. They quickly find themselves in "helper mode" and try to give others what they actually need themselves. And so, there is an urgent need for energy-based teachers who teach and support purely and clearly and encourage people to first look at themselves and work through things within themselves.
You end up in certain situations and certain people until you have permanently cleaned up and resolved things. And you can shorten your journey significantly by being very conscious and careful. You, with yourself.

Yet, we have deviated somewhat from the topic of suppressed feelings.

The behavior of suppressing emotions described above protects the respective environment to a certain extent (from outbursts of anger, for example) and that in and of itself is to be valued. However, every highly developed person still grasps it, even if the feelings are neither shown nor expressed or even acted out.
You know. And sometimes you also know that it was you who triggered the negative feelings.

From an energy-based perspective, there are forms of energy between the two of you at this moment. If you consciously give them space (within yourself) without handing over power to them, they can show themselves authentically and then dissolve sustainably. If you then speak matter-of-factly (something just made you angry, for example), you encourage the other person to verbalize, thereby consciously connecting with their well-being and thus achieving authentic self-empowerment. Your counterpart can now explore within themselves the reason for their anger and then formulate it calmly and matter-of-factly externally and so, you can resolve it together on a human-material level.

Yet, you can only live the behavior described if the energy form is not obscured in your own energy space. If there is still anger there in some way (repressed and not worked through), the energy form of your counterpart connects with yours, the energy form between you is suddenly and unexpectedly very huge and strong and you both now run the risk of being shaped by it and to act them out. From an energy-based perspective, this will cause you to dissolve in the long term, but on a human level you will usually cause yourself damage and so, acting out is clearly not advisable.

**Dealing with energy requires
a strong holistic stability.**

You can deal constructively with any form of energy as long as you have the necessary holistic stability. And so, holistic stability is not just an energy-based need, it is also a basic requirement for successful work with energies.

Regardless of what energies surround you: you need a strong and stable holistic foundation that offers you sustainable holistic stability, if you want to deal with energies in a beneficial way or even consciously change them in a positive way. If you basically have this, you can deal calmly and confidently with those you continually encounter. If you lack an internal, stable foundation, you will need external stabilization in a situation in which the energies become strong in order to be able to deal with the energies in a beneficial way. In the topic just discussed, this means: A person needs a stable and strong inner foundation. If he has this, he can remain calm even when things become restless internally or externally.

In relation to the example just described, this means: If strong forms of energy suddenly stand between you and you are tempted to act them out, the first step is to consciously stabilize yourself holistically. Feel the soles of your feet, breathe consciously into your stomach and consciously ensure that you become calm within yourself.
Strong negative feelings often cover (old) injuries. And once you have become calm inside, consciously connect with your current feeling and listen to them.
In order for you to do this, you must be internally stable. This stability, in turn, is based on a holistically healthy inner foundation.

If feelings flare up or negative feelings appear in a person, it would be wise to withdraw a little and clarify within themselves where the feelings come from.

And so, in said situation, retreat a bit and ask yourself:

- What's not going well right now?
- What are my feelings trying to point out to me?
- What should be different, here and now?

On a human level, authentic feelings are the most important inner navigation and people must learn to take this inner navigation very, very seriously. If people are in an open connection with their feelings and perceive their current state authentically and at the same time very seriously, they remain holistically stable from an energy-based perspective.

From an energy-based perspective, you remain stable when:

- You have consciously worked through all your previous injuries and thereby resolved them sustainably.
- You are consciously in your respective here and now.
- You consciously always perceive your authentic here and now feelings and take them seriously.

And if you like, take the topic with you into your next few days and observe consciously. Once you have grasped it in depth and mastered it sustainably, you are able to support and teach others.

When a person begins to consciously deal with their authentic feelings, this automatically brings them into confrontation with structures, ideas, norms and human laws. Said conscious confrontation not only leads step by step to conscious self-empowerment, it also serves to consciously resolve aspects that are hostile to life in the human environment.

**Holistic stability is a
energy-based basic need and
this applies to install
independently in yourself.**

And if you like, put the book aside and allow a personal introduction to the topic through your own inner essential self. Allow yourself to be explained and let yourself be consciously guided so that you have fundamental, holistic stability afterwards.

Excursus: Forms of Energy

At this point, allow us to point out a specific fact in the area of forms of energy.

If two people with a very high fundamental vibration frequency meet and both carry the same negative form of energy within them, it will not take long before said form of energy will show itself. Humiliation, for example. Both parties are now suddenly aware of the issue very clearly. And if they are not aware of what is happening to them - from an energy-based perspective - it can happen that the two of them act out the form of energy in some way and thereby cause human damage to each other. When two people with a very high fundamental vibration frequency meet, they create - from an energy-based perspective - a high-vibration shared energy field. Said energy field:

- Carries the power to shift the astral body and biological body towards a sustainable congruence.
- Brings truth to light.
- Promotes the positive life-enhancing options of the next few weeks.
- Increases the fundamental frequency of the respective parties if it still needs to increase.

- Loosens forms of energy that are still obscured and thus offers the opportunity to dissolve them sustainably. However, depending on the vibration frequency, said forms of energy can literally explode and so, this story requires a certain level of awareness.

If two people with a high fundamental vibration frequency meet and have the same negative form of energy in their personal energy space, they will suddenly find themselves confronted with a strong negative form of energy in their midst. A natural occurrence, viewed purely from an energy-based perspective.
However, most people are currently unaware of this. And so, both people benefit, if at least one of them is able to stabilize safely and sustainably and not become holistically addicted to the respective form of energy and thereby consciously refrain from acting it out. This requires awareness and discipline, but also the ability to remain calm at all times and to be able to stabilize yourself and your immediate surroundings safely and sustainably at all times. Skills, we strongly recommend you use.

3.2 Life-enhancing frequencies

The higher your personal basic vibration frequency rises, the more energy-based perception you will have. You begin to react intuitively to forms of energy, but also to frequencies. Very often, even before you are aware of it. It's a person's attitude that repulses you, for example. No matter how beautifully chosen his words are, you can still see the unattractiveness underneath.
Attitude and intention correspond to frequencies, viewed from an energy-based perspective. But family patterns, worldview, self-image, structures and norms are also very often underlaid with a certain frequency.
If you are mindful and aware, you will discover a lot of frequencies over time. Even in the materially based human habitat. According to energy-based evolution, vibration is above energy and energy is above matter. Therefore, the greatest power lies in the respective frequency.

The human habitat is permeated with frequencies that are hostile to life. And at the same time, people long for life-promoting and beneficial frequencies. Unconditional love, appreciation, respect, freedom from values, further development and freedom are, for example, such life-promoting frequencies.

The higher your own basic vibration frequency rises, the more you perceive frequencies that are hostile to life and the more you long for soothing and life-promoting frequencies.
At the same time, frequencies are now exerting an ever-increasing influence on you, your life and your practical everyday life and we would now, like to go into that.

When a child enters human living space, it is helpless and vitally dependent on other people. As a rule, it is lovingly and comprehensively cared for in the first few years of life and supported in continuing to develop and become independent. However, the human habitat is currently heavily polluted, and the years described are usually not without lasting damage.

One of them is embossing.
The type of setting in which a family lives shapes: the behavior, the thought patterns and beliefs, the view of the world and people. Said imprints can be perceived energy based as certain vibration patterns / complex frequencies and if they are consciously lived outside of you for a certain period of time, you have usually imposed them on your personal energy space in an unconscious way.

If your grandparents experienced war, were insecure for years, surrounded by a variety of suffering and poverty and were often not sure how to feed themselves and their children, they imprinted these frequencies into their children's energy spaces. Unconscious and yet. Their children grew up and fathered children of their own.
You for example. And while you lived with your parents, you were in sustained contact with the complex frequencies in question (including the corresponding basic human attitude) and now, have this imprint in your personal energy field. Yet, you will pass it on to your own children unless you are able to permanently dissolve said complex frequency.

If you are careful, you will be able to observe these patterns in some families. Poverty, addictions or even illnesses. Vibration patterns / complex frequencies that continue to shape without those affected being able to defend themselves.
Well, this is now changing more and more, as it is the same here as with the forms of energy in the respective personal energy space: As soon as they come into contact with high frequencies and stay that way for a certain while, the complex frequencies begin to loosen up, show up consciously and can thus be resolved sustainably.

On a human level, the issues associated with the complex frequencies come into the consciousness of the respective person and may be consciously lived out for a short time (alcohol, poverty), but one's own essential self remains in its power and is able to stabilize it holistically and the issue sustainably to dissolve. Every person with a high personal basic vibration frequency who meets the affected person and promotes the sustainable resolution of the complex frequency with their high frequency supports this. Every person with a fundamentally high vibration frequency is infinitely precious, therefore.

If you have consciously read the last pages of the book, you may have noticed that clarification work will increase over the next few decades and that many events in a person's life can now be assigned to this exact situation. It will be clarified. Sustainable and effective. Therefore, many events can no longer be classified in purely human cognitive terms and, in particular, it is no longer possible to draw any rational conclusions from them or even derive any predictions from them.

The goal is to effectively and sustainably clarify
your own energy space. Ideally, this happens
perfectly guided by one's own inner, essential
self and at the same time requires conscious and
disciplined work of resolution on the part of the
respective person.

The triggering situations come to you on their
own. However, you have to go through the
relevant work consciously. If you are mindful,
you will be able to identify the respective topics /
frequencies / attitudes in the setting into which
you have been drawn or in which you are
currently predominantly moving. Violence, for
example. Or even degradation. Abuse or denial
of personal responsibility, etc.
We encourage you to go through your everyday
life in the next few days with your eyes open and
pay attention to the topics and frequencies that
you encounter. And if you like, ask your own
inner essential self for guidance. By consciously
processing it, you will not only understand it
more deeply, you will also move more quickly on
the topic in question.

Every complex frequency in your personal energy space shapes you. The higher your own fundamental frequency, the more. At the same time, the level of your own vibration frequency also promotes its visibility and resolution options over time. However, the same applies here: you have to resolve it through conscious work. There is no way around it.

When you encounter life-enhancing frequencies, your entire being breathes a sigh of relief. You feel comfortable and would like to stay there. Over time, all highly developed, fully conscious people carry such life-enhancing frequencies within themselves and are able to keep them stable over a longer period of time. Peace, for example. If you discover such life-enhancing frequencies within you, we encourage you to give them space consciously and without intention. Consciously hold it stable and give them space, without intention and without forcing. Just let them take up space as long as it feels right and then things can change again.

While you carry said frequency within you, we encourage you to consciously observe:
- What does the frequency do within yourself?
- What effect does it have in your immediate environment?

Just notice and let your own inner essential self show you what you still need to know.

Life-promoting frequencies were among the energy-based basic needs. At the same time, you don't come across them too often in human habitat at the moment. However, you can repeatedly carry them within yourself, consciously give them space there and introduce them more and more into the human living space.

3.3 Natural orders

Susanne and her team have written several books on the subject of natural orders and if you want to delve deeper into them, we recommend this literature.

At this point, however, we would like to point out a few additional aspects that we also believe are important.

Natural orders are among the energy-based basic needs

And if you are connected to the energy-based dimension and subject to it and its circumstances and laws, you're longing for the full fulfillment of your energy-based basic needs becomes very strong. You now clearly perceive the artificial orders and you long for health in this regard. At the same time, the natural orders are very similar to the life-friendly frequencies: They begin within you and then, through you and your being, take up more and more space in the human living space.

If you like, take this topic with you into your next few days and if you perceive certain structures as unhealthy or artificial, allow yourself to perceive the counterpart of the healthy and natural in this area.

Natural orders are based on:
- Your free essential size
- Your authentic human needs and your human tasks
- Your essential needs and your current essential tasks
- Your energy-based needs

And if you like, we invite you again to the place we have prepared for you in the energy-based realm of the dragons. This is with the aim of talking to you about your personal here and now basic aspects of the natural orders.

Journey to the energy-based realm of the dragons
Retreat to an undisturbed, beautiful and quiet place, make yourself comfortable there and consciously breathe deeply in and out a few times. If you are then ready, allow yourself to be accompanied to the said location. You know when you're there. Take enough time to arrive safely and to orientate yourself consciously. You can see the same vibration-based building and are welcome to go inside and find the right place for you.

When you are ready, some dragons will join you and talk to you about your free essential size and your needs and tasks. Please express authentically and honestly what you have inside you right now and then just let it happen.
You know when it's complete. Thank you and say goodbye and return to your own place by making a conscious decision.
Once there, consciously stabilize yourself and rest a bit so that what you have just experienced can be integrated holistically.

You are still primarily human and so, your human needs and tasks have the highest priority.

- Your need for a pleasant place to live, food that is good for you, retreat, relaxation, sleep and exercise.
- Your need for beneficial human contacts and relationships, for love, intimacy, security, sexuality and tenderness, for personal development and stimulating conversations.
- But also, your need for protection and security, appropriate financial and material support, order and cleanliness, your right place in human society and the human tasks that are right for you.

All of your human needs are important and fulfilling them should continue to have a high priority in your everyday life. Something you will be able to observe effortlessly.

At the same time, your human tasks are still important and so, you will be able to see that no matter which global projects you are involved in, you always have enough space and time available for your respective human tasks. Ideally, you formulate internally what needs to be done in this regard and then, allow things to fit in as appropriate. You will also be able to observe this effortlessly. And once you realize and start to trust over time, your everyday life will continue to be optimally designed. The less you plan and organize, the more effortlessly and appropriately it will happen.

Your essential needs are based on your free essential size. In this area it is absolutely necessary that you can live your full potential and at the same time continuously develop yourself. Another important essential need is relationships and collaboration with people of the same size.
Yet, and the essential tasks take up space when you have successfully completed all the relevant preparatory work and you are completely ready for them.

The energy-based needs include healthy structures, free energy-based life and work, holistic stability and a fundamental feeling of being cared for in accordance with one's own essential size. But also, protection and knowledge of your own energy-based abilities and your own essential tasks. And, being authentically integrated into the bigger picture. The higher your basic vibration frequency, the more important the essential and energy-based needs and tasks become. And perhaps you have long been able to observe it in yourself: tasks that are fulfilling, that enable personal development, that strengthen you and in which you benefit the bigger picture are also part of the energy-based needs. It doesn't make you happy to just sit there and consume. On the contrary, the behavior described causes you to shrink and ultimately mummify.

3.4 Embedded in the big picture

People are not alone, and even if you have
gotten used to a certain feeling of being alone, in
the last few years, it shouldn't stay that way.
We have made enormous progress in the
"Project Earth", and so, we can now concentrate
in detail on ensuring that all members of the
project are well. Of course, this includes the
human material parameters, and these will now
be filled until you are comfortable everywhere.
Humans are "relationship creatures" and at the
same time, many highly developed people have
no longer been completely comfortable in
human relationships for a long time. That's why
we (members of Project Earth) are now very
consciously starting to network people of similar
size. On the one hand, it's good for you to have
contact with people who are like you. On the
other hand, in these contacts you can also try
out very practically how energy-based contacts
work, as your respective meetings are subject to
the energy-based dimension, just as you yourself
are.

Your contacts will be a little different as a result:
- They are transparent and authentic and sometimes people have to get used to them.
- The very thing that serves both of you is taking place. Therefore, there are exactly those topics in your midst that serve both of you.
- You don't have to plan it or design it consciously. They develop freely and to the highest and best of both parties.
- Look very consciously at yourself and work on what still needs to be worked on.
- The contacts will nourish you and enrich you in many ways. Something you don't necessarily know.
- They happen when you need them.

You are involved in a global project on a universal level. And once your human body is fully transformed into a light-based human body, you will very consciously repeatedly encounter other members of the project. By then, at the latest, you will understand the project more and more. Also, your own share in global events.
If you are currently in the process of converting your human body into a human light-based body, you will notice that your fundamental vibration frequency in particular will change significantly again.

You shine noticeably differently. As a result, you may also find that average people emit a frequency that energy-based personalities do not find very pleasant. To be honest, you are experiencing a very similar situation: the average "human frequency" is not only unpleasant, it also costs you a lot of energy.
The light-based human body is very clearly energy-based and so, you suddenly notice aspects that were previously hidden from you. Fast food feels downright disgusting, with the negative energies embedded in it and its low vibrational frequency, for example. Hotel beds become difficult because you capture all the energies and vibrational frequencies that are there.

The aspects described may have only accompanied you for a certain amount of time in your current human life, but if you then have a light-based human body, they suddenly appear very clearly and hugely in the room. A new challenge for which you need beneficial solutions.
You will find your own path that is good for you. At the same time, we would like to point out to you that you are now completely subject to the energy-based dimension, including its laws and circumstances. And here the rule is: you always have what you need.

So, please allow yourself to be guided very
consciously inside and observe. You will be
amazed to see that you can navigate effortlessly
and safely through the human environment and
always have what you need or what is good for
you.
Your needs are significantly different than those
of most people around you and we encourage
you to pay close attention to them and allow
yourself to recognize and find good solutions. If it
is right for you, let your own inner essential self
support you to understand it ever deeper.

Whatever you work on in this regard will not only
serve you but will also help you in the
aforementioned task of supporting highly
developed children with a very high vibrational
frequency. The children in question perceive
things based on energy and sometimes also on
vibrations. They pay attention to completely
different parameters than is usual among people.
Therefore, they primarily perceive the vibrational
frequency of their food and not necessarily the
taste or the physical health aspect. Your body
also constantly shows you what it needs and
when. And this incident alone requires parents
to be extremely conscious, as the issue of "food",
for example, can become a major challenge for
everyone involved.

If high-vibration frequencies are stable and high, they are beneficial for every living being. And if children or adults are able to keep their own high frequency stable, they involuntarily attract living beings. Animals, people and even plants become calm and comfortable in their surroundings. At the same time, however, any injuries that have not yet been processed or personal issues that have not yet been resolved also involuntarily become apparent.

Something that can be visibly destabilizing and can be easily observed, especially in small children. And so, everyone benefits if every person who carries a high vibration frequency is able to stabilize effortlessly and generously. The children described do not need a special lesson; they learn solely from you as a practical role model. If you are able to stabilize safely at any time, said children will involuntarily modeling this ability. And we probably don't need to tell you how incredibly precious this one fact alone is.

If you have a completely transformed light-based human body, you no longer have to worry about attitude. You are. Light and love. Stable and safe. No external factor can influence it anymore. It is now your stable frequency that basically has an influence: wherever you move.

If you feel within yourself that the transformation of your body into a light-based human body is now coming to an end, we encourage you to consciously pause and ask your own inner essential self for a comprehensive introduction.
If you have a light-based human body, you are subject to completely different laws and circumstances and you need to be fully aware of this.

**Allow clear awareness
who you are and what you accomplish.**

In the human environment, pioneers and those people who are at the top of the hierarchy often lead a lonely, sometimes even austere and withdrawn life. They invest extensively and intensively and only receive a fragmentary amount in return, as the others often do not yet understand what the pioneers have within them. Therefore, the immense benefits of their efforts are often discovered decades after their death, and it may well be that you intuitively expect something similar when you think about your future tasks.

Well, in the energy-based dimension things are different. Here everyone who carries out high and important tasks is particularly supported and valued. And of course, whatever they put in goes generously back to them.

This, in turn, behaves significantly differently than is usual or expected in the human living space and so, it will help you in this aspect if you consciously let go of all your ideas about this and just as consciously let your own inner, essential self introduce you to the topic.

You have to understand in order to be calm and to trust. This in turn is based on your own inner security and knowledge. Hardly anyone outside will be able to explain or show you this at the moment. And what you sometimes perceive as a disadvantage is actually an enormous advantage: it throws you back on yourself. You have to rely on your own inner self and over time you become incredibly independent and self-empowered because of that very fact.

In the human environment, every person can declare themselves big and powerful and sometimes receive a lot of money for an action that is definitely very small. The appearance works. Still. In the energy-based dimension, truth emerges fairly quickly, and it gets clear what actually is.

And if you feel within yourself that you have experienced some injustice in the area of the two aspects mentioned in your life so far, allow conscious clarification and lasting resolution and then, complete truth and your transparent essential size.

You don't have to declare your essential size or explain it to anyone. It only has to be free and authentic.
You will experience that you are particularly embedded on an energy-based level. Explicitly because of your precious size. At the same time, who you really are is now becoming more and more apparent in the human environment. Allow it consciously, knowing that you are well embedded in the energy-based dimension and are under its complete protection.
Perverted human behaviors can no longer truly affect you, although you will still encounter them. Unfortunately. This will probably stay that way for a while. But you will notice; At the latest when you have a light-based human body, the negative and unsightly things roll off you like rain on a raincoat. You now notice it much more clearly and at the same time, it affects you much less. Something that you probably have to experience for yourself to understand.

4. Your individual needs

If you like, pause for a moment and notice your authentic here and now needs. Unfiltered and value-free. And if you like again, then consciously give them non-judgmental space within yourself. Allow them to develop into your highest and best. No more and no less.

People are often not very connected to their authentic here and now needs. And if they then, notice them, they are very quickly in their head. There, in their human mind, they first filter and reflect, discard or plan and thereby unconsciously, mentally move away from their needs. They "water down" from an energy-based perspective, because from an energy-based perspective, the behavior described changes the respective frequency. It is no longer authentic and as a result it has clearly lost its power. Something that people are usually not aware of, as they have so far moved in a material-based living space and the rules apply there.

In human society, there exist many ideas of "energetic manifestation / realization". Many of them focus on mental versions and from a purely energy-based point of view it could be clearly shown for some of them why what should work can only work relatively, according to the established reality.

If you then, are subject to the energy-based dimension, you would do well to deal with the topic of energy-based manifestation / realization in great detail again and to be very conscious of seeking and recognizing truth. You are now subject to the energy-based dimension with its circumstances and laws, even if you still live in the material-based human habitat. Therefore, you become increasingly reliant on the ability of conscious energy-based manifesting as you now realize more and more in an energy-based way.

Energy-based manifestation is based on complete authenticity and your authentic here and now needs. Both parameters are not considered particularly important in human living space. On the contrary: it has to look beautiful or seem appropriate from the outside and the needs of society, the company, partner or children have to take precedence over your own needs. People are taught to put the needs of others before their own. As a result, many people are not authentic very often and are not consistently connected to their authentic here and now needs. However, if they are then subordinated to the energy-based level, both aspects are absolutely necessary so that their lives can continue to develop in a beneficial and appropriate manner.

And if you like, we invite you on a detailed journey through the topic together.

- What are you feeling right now, here and now?
- What are your authentic here and now needs?

Journey to the realm of the dragons

Retreat to a nice, quiet and undisturbed place, make yourself comfortable there and consciously breathe deeply in and out a few times. If you are ready, allow yourself to go to the place in the realm of the dragons that has been prepared for the readers of this book. You know when you're there. Take enough time to arrive safely and then go to the familiar building-like structure on your left. Walk to the back left and find your right place in the room there.

You will probably now be able to perceive mood, colors, tones, vibrations and different frequencies. If it feels right for you, consciously accept and allow. What surrounds you now was developed explicitly for you and your current situation, with the aim of connecting you even more deeply, with your respective authentic feelings and needs and thereby enriching your life sustainably. You'll know when it's complete.

Thank you and say goodbye and return to your own place by making a conscious decision. Once there, consciously stabilize yourself and rest a bit so that what you have just experienced can be integrated holistically.

The higher your personal vibration frequency rises, the more truth emerges. Suddenly you can no longer act "as if" and all of your previous coping mechanisms begin to slip away, only to dissolve completely over time. You can no longer say what isn't there. You can no longer do what is not your job.

When you start to discover the change described, it understandably scares you at first. Your previous behavior has helped you fit in and has therefore protected you to a certain extent. Now they are literally slipping away from you, and you involuntarily feel defenseless. You can't imagine how good things can develop in this way, in your front. In the human environment you find yourself exposed to all sorts of unpleasant things as soon as you don't fit in. Yet, you can't imagine that you should be safe in the human habitat without this important behavior. Well, you are now subject to the energy-based circumstances and their laws. This causes behavior to be significantly different than what your human mind can imagine.

Therefore, we recommend that you consciously stay calm, consciously refrain from creating mental constructs and instead, consciously allow all your authentic feelings and thereby dissolve them. Afterwards, continue to observe calmly and you will realize that your fears are not realized.

It's only you who knows. Everyone else won't notice the change that's so obvious to you. The outside fits in effortlessly without you having to act consciously. And so, it may help you, if you consciously refrain from doing too much and instead allow yourself to be introduced to the new situation by your own inner essential self.

At the same time, more and more things that no longer suit you are moving away from you. Sometimes settings and people who were very familiar to you and to some extent also dear to you, as they accompanied you for a long time and made up a large part of your life. Sometimes, however, also settings and people with whom you have tried for years to fit in and to please.

You can't hold on and part of you knows this. It slips away from you, and you seem to lose without knowing what will replace what is gone. You need a lot of inner strength and courage to endure the time described. However, you also need a stable and secure connection with your own inner essential self.

And we highly recommend that you consciously strengthen this connection and very consciously repeatedly seek inner dialogue with your own inner essential self. Speak truth and clarity about situations where you don't know what to do. Consciously ask yourself questions and allow yourself to fully understand. As challenging as the time described feels, you will also learn a tremendous amount for your future during this phase. You become secure in yourself, and you grasp and recognize. Increasingly. Differently than thought.

You can no longer make yourself fit and you can no longer disguise yourself and pretend to be small and inconspicuous. Your behavior in this regard dissolves without you being able to influence it, and what no longer fits slips away from you. The situation again triggers a lot of fear and here too you have to endure your fear, worries and negative mental scenarios to some extent. Whenever possible, by consciously giving space to all feelings and thus dissolving them sustainably.

The situation described takes you to a new country, metaphorically speaking. Your life becomes true and authentic. All of this feels like a loss and at the same time, a few years later, you will be amazed at how big your gain in this regard was.

Your human mind cannot imagine good solutions, and this causes a lot of fear and great uncertainty. Your previously important coping behavior is no longer effective. You are now connected to the energy-based dimension and things are different here. You can no longer find the answers to your questions and insecurities outside or in your human mind, but rather within yourself and in your essential self.
Yet, in the conscious inner confrontation with your front, your authentic feelings and needs begin to show more and more and this can trigger fear again, as some needs seem to be too big and too unrealistic. And also, during this time, we encourage you to consciously stabilize yourself, to keep your human mind calm and to consciously and calmly give space to all feelings within yourself. This is primarily an inner story that you make up with yourself. Until you feel calm and safe inside of you and your front is pure and clear. In yourself.

People often think they have this or that need. At the same time, needs are also very consciously shaped by the media, marketing strategists, politicians, etc. and so, they are often externally controlled without people being aware of it. If a person's vibration frequency begins to increase more and more, relevant influences and external influences can be increasingly recognized and then dissolve over time in the respective personal energy space.

The vibrational construct that you experienced on your last visit to the realm of the dragons was created explicitly for you in your current situation. It serves you to permanently dissolve the residual imprints that are still clouded in your personal energy space. So, don't be surprised if one thing or another becomes clear to you again in the next few days and weeks.

If it feels right for you, consciously allow your own inner essential self to bring you very clearly into contact with your respective authentic here and now feelings and your authentic here and now needs.
Pay conscious attention to your respective strategies for dealing with your feelings and needs. You have covered up, appeased, glossed over, not taken seriously, etc. many times and all of this may now consciously show itself again in the next few weeks and months so that you can grasp it and resolve it sustainably. At best, you will encounter repeated fears because you are not yet used to being completely authentic at all times. Your previous strategies often served your personal protection or security and if you lose them little by little, this can trigger feelings of defenselessness and insecurity.

We recommend that you consciously engage with everything that presents itself to you. Giving space and consciously working on it. Over time, you will notice that your inner security grows parallel to the external protective shells that are breaking away. A security that lets you be calm, even without external protective coverings. Something that you probably have to experience practically to understand in depth.

From an energy-based perspective, your authentic needs consist of a corresponding vibrational frequency. If the frequency is pure, clear and stable, it will move into your life accordingly. And you only have to consciously experience this several times in order to grasp it. You will be able to see that it happens in the best possible way and that it forms effortlessly and beneficially for everyone in the respective environment. Something you could never organize on a purely human level.

If you like, let your own inner essential self consciously introduce you to the topic so that you understand comprehensively.

4.1 Security is crucial

From an energy-based perspective, you are safe when you have an open and stable connection with your own inner essential self, and it is in control of your life. This automatically frees you from the external orientation that is currently common among people (including related dependencies) and strengthens your self-empowerment.

The ability to know safely and clearly at all times is also a crucial basic aspect in relation to your holistic security. The human living space is filled with all kinds of fictions and attempts at manipulation and people themselves act in a variety of ways with projections and overlays. If you cannot differentiate reliably at all times, you have neither self-empowerment nor holistic security. You are repeatedly at the mercy of your outside world as long as you do not always know clearly and securely within yourself and instead look for guidance within yourself. If you want to have a holistically secure life, you have to realize the corresponding security within yourself. This security, in turn, is not only central to your personal well-being, but also to your essential work.

If you feel within yourself that you are not yet
holistically confident, we encourage you to ask
your own inner essential self for guidance in this
regard. And if you encounter situations in which
you are not sure, consciously express clarity and
truth about them and allow it to be shown
accordingly. Then, put your full attention into the
energy field of the situation and consciously
perceive it. Until you know for sure.

Well, by consciously dealing with your authentic
here and now feelings and your authentic here
and now needs, you will probably realize that
these two aspects also play a very important role
in the area of holistic security. Because here too,
people are systematically taught to focus on their
outside world and to orient themselves there.
It's about fitting in, to serve society and comply
with all rules and norms. However, this is
repeatedly in direct opposition to you, your
current here and now, your authentic feelings
and your authentic needs.

Seen from the outside, it's an own story.
Everyone is aware of the topic to some extent
and yet, someone who is able to suppress their
own feelings and needs as much as possible is
stylized as a hero / heroine. Elite sport, for
example, is based, among other things, on said
ability. An ability that no one questions, although
it can be formulated as conscious violence
against oneself.

As a human being, you are taught to put yourself aside. If you are then, subject to the energy-based dimension, you must consciously learn to put yourself at the center. Different than what humans think because it is energy based. And you first have to recognize and grasp this in order to understand - once again - that the material-based dimension and the energy-based dimension are two completely different dimensions (and I, Susanne, formulate in human words that are usually used for the material-based dimension energy-based things, what is completely different and can usually not put into human words). In order to grasp the energy-based level, you absolutely need your own expanded energy-based perception ability. Otherwise, it reads "Chinese" and cannot be understood.

The described behavior of "putting yourself at the center" does not mean that from now on you fundamentally no longer fit in or are unable to fit in and serve society. It is just the mode of life that fundamentally changes once you are subordinate to the energy-based plane. And since the said mode of life will no longer change, it is important to study it in detail and use it consciously. Within the context of the materially based human living space, of course.

You manifest through your authentic here and now state of being.
And you usually don't find this feeling in your human mind. Some people are used to looking for all the answers in their heads. Also, the answer regarding his authentic here and now state of being, for example. And so, many people have to consciously learn to recognize where and how they can find the authentic answer regarding their here and now state, their here and now feelings and their here and now needs.

Do you know it?

If not, put the book aside for a while and let your own inner essential self guide you in this regard. Once you have definitely found the answer to the question above, allow yourself to be stable from now on, with your authentic here and now state of being and your authentic here and now needs.

Your front develops – on an energy-based level – from your authentic here and now. If you are completely connected to yourself, you always know what you need and how. If this is not the case, please consciously enter into an inner dialogue and allow the truth in this regard to show itself to you.

If you like, concentrate consciously on your current moment, give them completely space and perceive very consciously. Allow everything to show itself to you, especially with regard to yourself: the good and what suits you and what doesn't feel good. The more honest you are, the more empowered you will be from an energy-based perspective. If you also feel that you are still caught up in the typically human behavior of "imagining ahead," and if it feels right to you, allow for comprehensive clarification in this regard too. You know your future sufficiently well in advance and otherwise you are always sufficiently prepared for what comes your way.

There is currently a lot of "selling" in the human environment and this behavior is usually associated with manipulation. In addition, there are many, sometimes strongly nourished, fictions in human society about what a person needs or what is important in order to be able to take his or her place.
There are also projections and overlays, and you have to be very aware of this at all times. So, check very carefully. Over and over again. Especially when someone outside tells you what is right for you or when you realize that your own human mind is trying to develop images and ideas of your front.

Your navigation and your security lie within you and during a certain transition phase it will help you, if you become aware of this repeatedly. Pay attention to your authentic feelings and your inner clarity. If there are doubts and insecurities, take them very seriously and consciously work on them within yourself until you are clear and certain. This is also a behavior that has so far been rather unusual among people and at the same time it is centrally important for all those who are now subject to the energy-based dimension. You are not safe as long as external influences are able to shape you and so, you will be guided through personal training sessions until you have mastered the topic sustainably.

Your general well-being increases significantly as soon as you consciously pay attention to the right here and now.
And if you like, consciously take the topic with you into your next few days. Direct your focus on your own here and now state. Be very careful and conscious of yourself. Even and especially when you are with other people. If you are comfortable, the others are too. If your here feels holistically good for you, you have the people around you who are right for you.

You will probably have to consciously experience it a few times before you realize how important the aspect described is once you are subject to the energy-based dimension. It is your authentic here and now frequency that shapes. It shapes significantly.

If you continue to observe, you will increasingly realize that you are continuously manifesting using said frequency. Thought, taught or imagined differently than human materially based and yet incredibly effective.

- You don't have to imagine what would be good for you now, your authentic frequency is constantly realizing.
- You no longer have to organize your tomorrow because you will continue to realize tomorrow in the same way. The one that then serves you. Something you can't really know yet.
- It continuously forms according to your respective authentic here and now frequency and so, you no longer have to "think up" or work out many solutions for certain challenges; rather, they fall to you continuously.

Yet, the same applies here: you have to have practical experience several times in order to understand it in depth. The process described is significantly different than what you are used to as a material-based person.

Your safety is central and if you are not yet where you should be on this topic, consciously allow yourself to recognize where you still have to work on. You won't get anywhere unless you're completely confident on your own. And that's what you need to be aware of.

4.2 A completely essential life

The materially based human living space is filled with norms, rigid structures, laws, people who have power over you, influences, manipulations and overlays and this makes individuality largely impossible. Rather, it makes it impossible to search for one's own essential self and to live a life that corresponds to one's inner being. This is not required and usually not desired in current human society. And at the same time, many people carry exactly this longing within themselves. Even if they would perhaps put it in slightly different words. However, as long as they are subject to the material-based dimension, this is only relatively possible, as they are therefore subject to all relevant norms, laws, etc.

Therefore, they must first master the material-based dimension sustainably, harmonize the law of duality and then, increase their own basic vibration frequency to such an extent that their holistic being connects to the energy-based dimension. Before that, an authentic, essential human life is not possible in the human habitat.

The materially based human habitat has made many different experiences possible, so far. At the same time, most of these experiences were neither beneficial nor empowering. On the contrary, most of these experiences have burdened and weakened people in the long term and dampened personal vitality. Not only did people themselves become increasingly sick, the human habitat and the entire planet also began to suffer from the increasing negativity. Therefore, you are one of the last generations to still experience the diverse, stressful experiences of the human environment. In the next few centuries this will change significantly and many of the previous experiences will no longer be possible.

Item: What we describe in this chapter is deliberately aimed at those people who are already connected to the energy-based dimension. Because as already described; As long as a person is still subject to the material-based dimension, a truly essential life is not possible.

If you lead a life that meets your essential needs and in which you can use your essential skills, this will keep you holistically healthy.

If you lead a life according to your free essential size and live your essential tasks, you will be fulfilled and satisfied. This, in turn, corresponds to a certain frequency from an energy-based perspective and if you carry this frequency stably within you, it is continuously formed according to this frequency in your practical everyday life.

- You are rich.
- You are fulfilled.
- You are satisfied.
- You are healthy.
- You are sure and safe
- You continue to develop with curiosity and openness.

And what we are formulating here cannot be organized on a human, mental, material basis. Here too, you have to get to know the energy-based mode and understand it in depth. In order to then consciously give it space and use it consciously.

At the same time, you will encounter a lot of restrictive norms, structures, human ideas, beliefs and limitations. You will realize how extremely damaging the issue of performance and focusing on success is.

And you will realize that these are forms of
energy that are currently woven into most
human energy spaces. Forms of energy that
restrict and burden. Forms of energy that
dampen liveliness.
You will probably also realize how damaging it is
when you have to meet standards that others
define (for you). In these situations, you cannot
make a significant contribution or act freely.
Therefore, it cannot happen for the highest and
best of all those involved, and this frustrates you
once you reach a certain level of awareness, as
you intuitively know within yourself that
significantly more could have happened if you
had been allowed to act freely.

People are currently being massively prevented
from discovering their true selves, from being
able to shape their true lives and from
developing and using their true potential.
However, most people are not yet aware of this.
Human society limits people and human life. In
principle.
And if you are a person with a high essential size,
you feel these limitations in almost every area of
your life. It's rubbing inside and you're not
feeling well. Never, actually. Because you cannot
live according to your true nature. Something
that isn't good for you.

Once, your holistic being has become connected
to the energy-based dimension, it also begins to
change in the area of practical life and shifts
more and more towards a holistically essential
human life.
A life that unfolds freely according to your
essential size and your authentic needs. A human
life that essentially corresponds to you in all
areas. You will clearly notice the difference from
before.

An essential life includes the fact that you can
bring in all of your great potential and thereby
make an impact according to your essential size.
An essential life is deeply individual. It can
therefore neither be prescribed nor taught or
even conducted or evaluated externally. An
essential life is under the guidance of one's inner
essential self.
This means that the open conscious connection
with one's essential self is central. This too
cannot be imposed or even brought about
externally, but it can certainly be supported in a
variety of ways. A topic that is described in detail
in many other books by Susanne and her team.

4.3 Inner leadership

In the course of the personal awareness process, the leadership of your life changes. Your human self (and your human spirit) is losing their power and the power of your inner essential self is increasing step by step. At some point, you reach the point of your own inner essential self fundamentally taking over the leadership and control of your whole life, and this situation is not that easy to bear, as it is accompanied by a very strong feeling of loss of control. Your human self loses control and this triggers repeated fear and panic. At the same time, you feel very clearly that you can't go back. It pushes you forward, and you have to consciously surrender and trust. The quicker you do this, the quicker you will become stable again. And you will realize that you will not sink or lose.
And even if you grasp it very quickly, it still takes some time until you find your way around the new place and feel comfortable.

If you pay attention, you will realize that your inner self is constantly communicating with you. This is an inner clear knowledge. You know that your current job is about to end, for example. There are no external parameters in this regard and yet you know. Pure and clear. And we strongly encourage you to consciously allow yourself to now learn to find your own good way of dealing with this form of communication.

Because this one inner knowledge does not contain any external call to action and so, you don't have to study any job advertisements. Rather, you know that change will happen, and you have to consciously carry this within you. In doing so, you will only be able to record the associated processing orders yourself. Certain fears or sadness, etc.

If you are open and attentive, you know the associated inner processing topics just as clearly within yourself as the respective inner information. Once you have finished editing, you can continue. As a rule, you know very early on and therefore have enough time to solve all the associated work on your own on an ongoing basis. At the same time, you have to consciously learn not to act externally too early and thereby force things.
A person is usually very action-oriented and if it is internally clear, he acts accordingly. However, things are now changing fundamentally, and so, inner clarity no longer necessarily means involuntary implementation on the outside. Rather, it is a first sign for yourself. Usually at a very early stage. You know, and at the right time it will also be outside. Without you consciously changing or forcing it. Rather, by consciously allowing and continually doing what you know within you to be pure and clear impulses for action.

Very often you do things in completely different areas and yet things change in a wonderfully appropriate way. Effortless and soothing.

You can consciously support the challenging and sometimes even stressful time of "taking over internal leadership" by consciously getting involved and letting go of control. Also, learn to recognize your inner essential voice as quickly as possible and consciously observe and examine it a few times so that you can trust it more and more. Once you have consciously built up said trust, it becomes easier within yourself.
If the trust described is then more or less established, your practical human life will not only move very quickly in the direction of your personal essential life, it will also very quickly take shape outside of your previous ideas and thereby trigger fear, doubts and concerns again and again. And if you like, we invite you to visit us again in the realm of the dragons.

Journey to the realm of the dragons
Retreat to a nice, quiet and undisturbed place, make yourself comfortable there and breathe in and out consciously and deeply a few times. If you are ready, allow yourself to be accompanied to the said place. You know when you're there. Take enough time to arrive well holistically. Enter the "building-like structure" you are already familiar with, move up to the second floor and go to the right side. There are some dragons waiting for you. Go to them, settle down and then tell them what you currently have inside you. Then enter into a conscious dialogue with the dragons and let them consciously support you in your current situation. Until you feel that this meeting is complete.
Thank you and say goodbye and return to your own place by making a conscious decision. Once there, consciously stabilize yourself and rest a bit so that what you have just experienced can be integrated.

If your essential tasks begin to take up more space in your practical everyday life, you will repeatedly find yourself in situations that you are unable to solve with your previous coping strategies. You need new behaviors and, purely theoretically, you could find out about them through various experiments.

However, we need you urgently and far too much valuable time would be lost with the behavior described. Therefore, we would like to consciously support you in developing helpful solution strategies for your new challenges.

When your essential tasks begin to take up more space in your practical human everyday life, things change significantly.
Your previous human everyday life is losing strength and instead your day is continually forming. From this moment on, you can no longer lead a "normal human" life. And you waste a lot of time and energy, if you try to do this repeatedly. You can no longer say exactly what your tomorrow will look like. Maybe you have some fixed dates that you know will happen, but the rest will continue to develop harmoniously. According to you and your authentic needs.

If you now consciously let go internally and begin to observe just as consciously, you will be able to see that your new way of life is not particularly noticeable to anyone on the outside and that it fits effortlessly into the respective human settings. It is only you who knows and it is important to be very aware of this.

The change described, even if it fits in effortlessly is not noticed by anyone else. Yet, it is still a profound change and needs to be consciously recorded, consciously understood and consciously processed.

This requires a strong and secure connection with your own inner essential self and your complete trust in your own inner guidance. If you begin to consciously observe, the change of mode described does not necessarily mean professional independence or a life without a partner and children. Your new way of life will also take place in the middle of an employment relationship and in a family setting. At best, you may behave a little unusually repeatedly, but you will notice that the people around you only notice this relatively quickly and then quickly forget it. You, however, you recognize. And you would do well to continually formulate in a very conscious inner dialogue what irritates you or makes you insecure.

It is your inner clear guidance that now continually informs you about the important aspects of your front. And it helps you if you consciously step out of your human thinking and no longer try to find mental solutions. Instead, it will continue to evolve. For the highest and best for you and your surroundings.

You will have to consciously endure this a few times until you get used to it and can trust calmly and confidently from now on. Your front is increasingly viewed in a more unusual, purely human way, and so, you must be able to trust your own inner essential self to be safe and stay safe.

**You are then, most successful,
if you go along with the one
that is here and now without expectations,
and at the same time, let consciously
develop to the highest and best
of all those involved.**

At a certain point, you have to fundamentally rely on your own inner guidance. In this phase you can no longer mentally solve what is coming to you in a humane way. You don't have to do that anymore. Instead, consciously engage with your own inner guidance and work within yourself until you know clearly and confidently.

Your challenges are now becoming more complex step by step, as you now, seem more and more aware of social and global issues. As a result, you can neither classify things mentally nor solve problems mentally. Therefore, you have to (be able to) rely completely on your own inner guidance. If you are not there, yet consciously allow to see what you still need to consciously work through in order to get to the point you want. You can't go any further until you've mastered the topic sustainably.

And even though you are now embarking on your first global projects, and these will increase in size and complexity over time, your complete well-being is still the most important criterion in your practical everyday life. And it will stay that way. However, your holistic care is different than humanly expected and so, you may have to broaden and change your perspective a little so that you also understand this fact.

5. Self-empowerment

The further you move outside of what is normal for humanity, the more self-empowerment has to become an issue: in your human consciousness and of course also in your very practical everyday life. However, the human environment consists of a lot of dependencies, and this means that as a human being you are used to living in a very limited form of self-empowerment. What's more, over the course of a human life you repeatedly learn that you lose (a lot) when you move away from human dependencies and as a result you tend to stay in them. In addition, you are taught to be dependent and therefore fundamentally do not trust yourself to have complete self-empowerment. This seems to be beyond human reach and sometimes beyond thought reach.

From the outside, people never really grow up. They trust other people more than themselves and they systematically give up responsibility. Responsibility that they should actually bear themselves. Many of these behaviors occur unconsciously. Lived and shaped many times on the outside and never consciously questioned. People move away from their actual here and now incredibly quickly. Sometimes distracted unconsciously. Very often, however, also more or less consciously "running away". Often very subtle and internal.

But that doesn't make it any less true. A human life is an incredibly strenuous and challenging affair, and many people refuse to take complete responsibility for themselves and very consciously shape their own life.
If you begin to observe in the way described, you will be able to observe a large number of unfortunate human life strategies. And if it feels right for you, consciously allow your own unfortunate human life strategies to become apparent to you (if there are still any). So that you can consciously process and resolve them.

Holistic care, safety and protection are important aspects of a human life. In the human environment, you get these aspects, especially in group settings, and this involuntarily leads to a person repeatedly finding themselves in these settings and the associated dependencies.
The average person is currently still convinced that holistic care, security and protection cannot be carried out completely alone and living independently is not possible in the human living space (which is true to certain extent). And so, most people arrange a life surrounded by a variety of dependencies, get used to it and live with it.

Complete self-empowerment does not seem possible as a human being. And yet, part of your being longs for it. In addition, self-empowerment is part of your essential power and the higher your vibration frequency rises, the greater the longing for self-empowerment becomes. However, self-empowerment only seems to be possible in a very limited form, in the human environment and if you move outside of the general norm, you usually lose (quite a lot). So, how can self-empowerment succeed in the midst of human society without losing out? We would like to deal with this in this chapter.

Financial support, being integrated into a community, but also protection and security, seem to be hardly possible in a pure form in the human environment because it is not burdened with all sorts of dependencies and unpleasantness. Self-empowerment also seems to be only relatively possible as a human being and so, over time, you find your way of dealing with the situation. However, the higher your basic vibration frequency rises and the more your consciousness opens, the more the many dependencies within you begin to rub together. Inwardly, it pushes you more and more towards self-empowerment and a part of you longs for this in the sense of a fully essential life. Another part, however, "laughs at you". He has already tried a lot of things in this regard, has failed very often and has now given up to a certain extent.

Complete self-empowerment as a human being? This is not possible. You are exposed to all kinds of things and all kinds of people (police, judges, psychiatrists, bosses, teachers, etc.) are allowed to exercise power over you. You can twist and turn it; As an average person, you are usually pretty far away from actual self-empowerment.

However, if your holistic being is subject to the energy-based dimension and its laws, your possibilities in this regard begin to expand significantly. And so, you have to change levels in order to achieve actual self-empowerment.

5.1 Your power lies on the energy-based level

And there, on an energy-based level, there is authentic transparency at all times. In the energy-based dimension you can only have the power that is essentially yours. In the area of your own life, but also in the area of social or global tasks. Every other personality experiences exactly the same thing. It is and happens according to the respective essential size. You cannot disguise yourself and you cannot exalt yourself. You are. The way you are.

As a person, you are not used to this and at first glance it seems rather dangerous to you, as you are not protected in this setting. At least that's what it seems to you. Therefore, you first have to observe carefully and slowly, until you understand the new and then, over time, can trust it.

Please be very appreciative and loving towards yourself at all times. Knowing that you are currently experiencing an incredible amount of new and unfamiliar things. Aware that the processing and adaptation required in this regard is immense and it is also normal that you will not be able to master everything immediately. Allow support and allow periods of rest. Repeatedly consciously allow everything that serves you here and now. May you have a time as good as possible, even in the midst of very high demands.

If your holistic being changes its connection and is now subject to the energy-based dimension, it is central that you consciously allow your essential size freely and openly and that you also consciously allow your essential power openly and freely. Something that you as a human being are usually not used to.

Power is often perverted in the human environment, many highly developed people have tended to avoid human power and so, it is quite possible that you will become aware of one or two related issues again as soon as you begin to move towards self-empowerment.

Energy-based forms according to your free essential size and thus your free essential power. You don't have to do anything outside. It happens. And if you like, we invite you to an experiment in this regard.

Go into a room with several people and consciously keep your free essential size and your free essential power stable. Hold the frequency and observe very consciously.

Then let your own inner essential self show you and introduce you comprehensively to the topic. If it feels right for you, do the exercise repeatedly. Until your essential size and your essential power are free at all times. And until you understand the topic in depth.
Your self-empowerment, your fundamental power and your personal holistic abundance are based on your free essential size, and this is significantly different than a human mind can imagine.

You have to grasp the topic on an energy-based basis. Full. So that you understand in depth and have mastered it sustainably. Something that you then know, pure and clear within you.

If a group that has to work or live together is restless, the hierarchy that exists there does not correspond to the essential hierarchy in the sense of the natural orders. This means that someone with a smaller essential size has the highest position in the hierarchy. If you are attentive, you will be able to observe that this group somehow cannot seem to calm down, regardless of what is being tried outside. If you put someone with a high essential size at the head of the group in question, it will automatically become quiet.

If a group is constantly restless or not very efficient, it can also be the case that the person who should have the highest hierarchical position due to their size and therefore their power refuses to take their natural, because essential, position. It is not good for a group to be led by a much smaller person. Not even if the person in question has official management training and is officially authorized externally for their management position.

At the latest when there is a person in the said group who is connected to the energy-based level, the energy-based evolution will clearly play a role in the topic and the group would now form freely and independently according to the respective essential size. However, this is usually not the case, and so, the system begins to constantly "rub" and the group members repeatedly feel uncomfortable, often without being able to formulate why.
Please check within yourself whether you have clarified all blocking issues regarding a freely lived power within you. If this is not the case, ask your own inner essential self to guide you in this regard.

Human society currently urgently needs people with a high essential size and a completely open consciousness in its leadership positions.
However, this is only possible if the people in question are open to these positions in their entirety.
On an energy-based level, you lead using your free, stable vibration frequency. You enter a group of people and keep your own vibration frequency pure and clear and stable. If all participants in this group do this, the hierarchy will involuntarily rearrange itself according to the essential size and actual abilities of the respective people.

It's clear, everyone knows. Without verbal exchange, without fighting, without any discussion. The positions and tasks are clearly and transparently distributed. According to the essential size and actual abilities of the respective people. At the energy-based level, there are no external allocations of power. It forms involuntarily according to the essential size and abilities of a personality. Different in every group constellation.
However, an exception also exists on an energy-based level: the conscious allocation of tasks and power by the Council of Light. But we don't want to go into that any further at this point.

Since you are subordinate to the energy-based level, we encourage you to consciously allow this energy-based natural condition to take up space in your life and to use it consciously. This in turn will have a healing and beneficial influence on any group in which you move. Thanks to your conscious behavior, energy-based evolution gains strength and shapes the respective setting. Of course, for the benefit of everyone involved.
If you like, take the topic with you into your next few days and observe and recognize in a very practical way so that you also understand this aspect in depth.

5.2 Your power is based on authenticity

The energy-based dimension is subject to different circumstances and different laws than the material-based dimension. And so, other parameters are important at this level. In the area of your power, the issue here is, among other things, complete authenticity. If you are completely honest, energy-based development can develop accordingly. And since, according to energy-based evolution, energy is above matter, this will automatically show up on a material-based level as well.
This requires, especially at the beginning, a conscious examination of oneself. Ideally, away from other people.

People are used to looking for (and finding) in others and outside what they actually need to look for (and find) within themselves. And so, at the latest when your holistic being has connected to the energy-based level, a conscious paradigm shift is worthwhile. Also, with regard to complete self-empowerment.
You can also manifest with your human self. However, your real power lies within your essential self. Where you cannot reach with your human will. Therefore, it requires your conscious surrender to your own inner essential self. A decision that is extremely difficult for many people.

At the same time, it is essential for your further progress, and you will then discover that your life will become incredibly effortless. If you are authentic in your here and now, you will continue to develop without you having to worry about what you will eat and when or how your evening will be. You are completely here and at the same time continually do what you know to be pure and clear impulses within you. A mode of life that needs to be consciously discovered and grasped. A way of life that very consciously leads you into complete self-empowerment.

Over time, you will find that it continues to evolve according to your authentic needs. You don't have to worry anymore. Not about the needs themselves and not about how you meet them. All that is required is your complete openness and complete honesty. After that, the things that serve you highest and best continue to happen to you.
This represents a slightly different form of self-empowerment than a human mind imagines. And so, here too, it is important to consciously expand your perspective and change something in order to then consciously grasp it. A grasp that lies far beyond the human mind.

6. Power

Once you have mastered the seventh dimension, your natural power is based on your free essential vibrational frequency. If you are one of those people who will have a light-based body and will therefore be connected to the ninth dimension, your natural power is based on light. Both aspects are based on an unprecedented event in the human environment. And so, you are a pioneer in this regard and experience all the corresponding joys, but also the corresponding challenges. We would be happy to accompany and support you in this area if you like. On the one hand, in the course of your discovery in this regard, but on the other hand, now, in the context of this book, in the form of helpful information.

6.1 Power based on your essential vibrational frequency

If you have mastered the vibration-based seventh dimension in this one human life, you know this internally pure and clearly. If this is not the case (yet), feel free to skip this chapter, as the words are not written for you. What we are now writing here applies explicitly to those people who have already successfully mastered the seventh dimension in this one human life. If this is the case, you have a very high level of purity, clarity and integrity. Most people can understand this somehow, but only to a very limited extent. On an energy-based level this is different: here it is obvious what is. And if you now meet other personalities in the energy-based dimension, they will involuntarily grasp your holistic development and they will just as involuntarily give you respect and honor. This happens differently than what humans are used to or thought and at the same time, it is a natural occurrence in the energy-based dimension. Please don't involuntarily close yourself off because you don't know this from your life so far but stand calmly and consciously and consciously accept.

Until now, you were often used to other, much smaller and usually more "incompetent" people being officially granted respect, appreciation and power. Most people are incapable of grasping truth and so, they worship all sorts of things and people. You have adapted to the discrepancy described and endured it within yourself. However, it wasn't natural and so, it caused a lot of internal friction and a lot of injuries. And if you feel a certain resonance with the words, put the book aside for a bit and consciously allow this to become clear to you and allow you to process and resolve it sustainably.

If you are at the described holistic level of development, you have great power.

If you consciously speak into a human life, it begins to order itself involuntarily.
This happens regardless of whether the person in question officially believes you, listens to you or understands you, questions you or devalues you. You speak out and it begins to move on an energy-based level. For the highest and best of the respective person or system.
Therefore, we ask you to very consciously take these lines with you into your next few days and to observe them very consciously.

You have often spoken the truth and then often internally reprimanded yourself because the person in question reacted to it in a defensive and often derogatory way. You questioned yourself and your words many times, even though a part of you clearly knew that you were speaking the truth. You didn't recognize yourself and didn't feel valued. On the contrary. And when you read the lines, you probably realize that there are still one or two things in this area that need to be consciously worked through and thus resolved within yourself. So that you can be completely free here too.

Well, with the approach described, your power is not in the human realm. Therefore, it is irrelevant how the affected person reacts. To be honest, it is beyond his personal human power to determine whether things will change accordingly. Please consciously change your perspective in this regard and let your inner, essential self consciously show you: Once you have expressed vibration-based what the respective person or the respective system needs for its holistic further development, it will involuntarily form accordingly.
First, only on an energy-based level and if you are attentive, you will grasp the respective energy-shift, involuntarily.

Afterwards also visible on the materially based human level. It is your pure and clear frequency that does the work. Involuntarily. Beyond human influence. And you have to understand this yourself.

You need a comprehensive understanding of the situation just described so that you can remain calm and in your strength after saying your words. This is ideally done through several practical experiences. If you are not aware of what you are doing and why, you allow yourself to be confused on the outside as a human being or confuse yourself through your own questioning and doubting. This in turn dampens the power of words and thus causes lasting damage. In yourself and in your counterpart.

You effect based on frequency(s)
If you enter a certain setting with a stable high frequency, negative and stressful forms of energy and energy fields begin to involuntarily loosen in the place itself, in the building and in the holistic systems of the respective people. It therefore becomes visibly negative, destructive and dark. Naturally and involuntarily. It loosens, shows itself and then dissolves permanently.

The people in question also begin to express or sometimes act out stressful overlays and projections that have become entangled in their holistic systems. Naturally and involuntarily. And so, it becomes chaotic, at times confusing and illogical and overall "dynamic" on an interpersonal level. If you are aware of this, you can consciously observe and speak and act calmly and confidently. Knowing that good things are happening in the long term, even if it definitely seems different on a human level. However, once you have consciously experienced the situation in question several times, you will understand it better and more confidently in the situation described. You are doing immense good and at the same time, it is happening significantly differently than the average person imagines "doing good".
From a vibrational perspective, logical. Human materially based viewed confused and illogical.

The calmer and clearer you are in the situations described, the greater the impact you will have. You can see this because the negativity and chaos will increase in intensity, and you may not be able to see the corresponding success personally. At the same time, however, a secure inner knowledge guides you.

Yet, many a time you still experience the corresponding result in each human life. Something that always helps you to consciously remain stable and calm in the respective situations. Knowing that what is happening now is right and good. You work vibration-based using high and pure frequencies and thereby promote sustainable clarification. From an energy-based perspective, things naturally become dark and negative at first.

At this point we would like to point out to you again that, from an energy-based perspective, the most effective option is to speak out or act out overlays in order to get rid of them permanently. If these are then permanently dissolved, they are no longer able to think or express themselves about the person in question. This means that you can often no longer take seriously what you say to other people or what they say. Sometimes it feels like truth at first and then involuntarily dissolves. And it will help you a lot if you are not only aware of this, but also increasingly recognize as quickly as possible that a situation now requires resolution work. Extremely important and valuable from an energy-based perspective. Unsteady and confusing from a purely human perspective.

6.2 Power based on light

If you have a light-based human body, you know this internally, purely and clearly. If so, what is written in this chapter applies to you personally. If this is not the case, the written words do not (yet) apply to you.
If you have a light-based human body, your power is based on light. This power cannot be controlled or used in any way. Power based on light is. And if you leave it free and open, it appears involuntary. Something that you probably have to experience practically in order to understand in depth. If you have a light-based human body, we recommend that you consciously allow light to take up space: in yourself, in your life and in your ongoing actions. You now have power that the average person cannot even begin to imagine, and you will now be able to observe this on an ongoing basis. You intuitively do the right thing, and you intuitively say the right thing. You have a high impact, even when you sit quietly in a corner.

Light has incredibly great power, and this will become very clear to you when your human body starts to transform into a light-based human body. Light shows truth. The higher a person's fundamental frequency, the faster truth becomes apparent.

Therefore, you know continuously. Sometimes things that the people affected themselves don't yet understand. You have trained this situation naturally over the last few years and are now able to deal with it without any problems.

If you have a light-based human body, what actually is, continually shows up in your own life. You know. And, you now know that you can trust this knowledge. This makes your human life much easier and at the same time the situation described enables "completely free hands and a completely free head". You no longer have to worry about many everyday things because things continue to develop harmoniously, and you always know in advance. You will now experience in full what you have been able to get to know step by step over the last few years (and sometimes had to, to be honest).

Well, you need your attention, your time and your energy for other things. Therefore, you still find yourself well integrated into human settings and lead a completely normal human life to the outside world, but at the same time you now work primarily social and global. In doing so, you will find yourself safely guided by your own inner essential self. Far away from any human mental constructs.

At the same time, what you have been carrying within you as knowledge for a long time will now become increasingly real. Most likely bigger and different than the image you had in your mind. And yet extremely suitable: for yourself, but of course also for the (high!) tasks that you will now continually carry out.

Allow and it will happen!